HONORING MY PARENTS:
A TRIBUTE TO
Mom and Dad
My best friends forever

SANDRA CHATOOR

**HONORING MY PARENTS: A TRIBUTE TO MOM AND DAD
MY BEST FRIENDS FOREVER**

Copyright © 2024 Sandra Chatoor.

All rights reserved. No part of this book may be used or reproduced by any means, graphic, electronic, or mechanical, including photocopying, recording, taping or by any information storage retrieval system without the written permission of the author except in the case of brief quotations embodied in critical articles and reviews.

Because of the dynamic nature of the Internet, any web addresses or links contained in this book may have changed since publication and may no longer be valid. The views expressed in this work are solely those of the author and do not necessarily reflect the views of the publisher, and the publisher hereby disclaims any responsibility for them.

ISBN: 978-976-8290-34-2 (sc)

Print information available on the last page.

Preface

This book is intended to activate an awareness ,to treasure and appreciate the love and sacrifices of our first teachers, protectors and strongest supporters in our lives, our parents. To acknowledge their contribution, time and effort in enlightening us with values by example that never diminishes with time. God's gift to us ,to support them unconditionally in their hour of need and to never give up. The words of my poems depict our lives together and my deep thankfulness to my mom and dad who asked for nothing and gave everything. My mom sustained a fractured hip and was confined to her bed for almost three years. She taught me the power of determination and perseverance and love. An avid reader whose knowledge was remarkable and could convincingly debate any topic. Her love of family unparalleled . She is so dearly missed. My dad was diagnosed with Alzheimer's for five years prior to 2022 and through the uncertainty of this devastating disease our closeness never wavered. If anything it brought us even closer. My dad loved to read also, made his own draught board to challenge his brain and always made sure we were okay. He encouraged us to be our best and showed us how much he cared. His sense of humor was legendary. He endured his suffering and never complained. He is my hero and I thank God for him and mom every day. I lost both my parents in 2022.

Mom

My heart is broken And you're not here
To mend it... You will live on In my heart
I don't know How I'm going To get
through The next few Days
And the rest Of my life
But I know that You're always Here for me
It seems so strange You're not calling me
I will never
Hear your voice again Right now
I cannot bear this feeling But somehow
I will get through Because you are My unseen strength
I love you so much mom... My life will never
Be the same And it still hasn't Hit me as yet
Things have changed In one instant
But God knows best And he's giving you A big welcome
Just about now...

Love always and forever San 13/04/2022

Mom

It's six months Today
since you left us...
And it seems like
Just yesterday... Your presence
still felt
So strongly... In my
every move My best friend
For life... My source of inspiration My confidant The keeper of
my well being Mom
I thank God For
giving me The best years
Of my life Spent with you... I'm truly Blessed...
I wish for you
Peace and Endless happiness...
Thank you God...
For fulfilling My wish...

I love you Mom

So very much...

San 13/10/2022

Mom

It is now eight months Today
Since you left me And I still
Am blinded by My tears... My life is
Filled with reminders That can never be Erased...
The memories Are deeply
Etched in my brain And my heart... You will forever
Be with me In spirit...
I thank God For you...
My sweet mom

Love San 13/12/2022

Mom

Today is nine months Since
I lost you And
I still count Each one... You are
so present
In my thoughts... My heart
still breaks When memories
Come flooding back...
I love you So much... Especially for caring
for me without reserve
You will always be
My best friend... No one else qualifies
Like you do... You took a piece
Of my heart with you...
we will always Be together Wherever
our lives And souls Take us
Dearest mom... Love always

San 13/01/2023

Mom

You endured so much And still stood tall… A pillar of
mental fortitude… Well read and knowledgeable
Someone to be reckoned with… An intellect and
a soft heart combined No one
excluded from your club
Your brand of welcome
And heartfelt caring… Stories of
your generosity and kindness Keep emerging…
You're one
of a kind mom… Your love
flows naturally Like a stream…
For us
Your ever loving children And strangers
alike… There is never going to be
a replica Of you mom When God
created you… There was no template

That could match your uniqueness…
You left But your star still twinkles… we love you
so much mom…

Love San 31/07/2023

Mom

I miss you so much My guiding
light My reason
for living… My strength And supporter
of my dreams… You propel me
forward
In this uncertain
world… You give me reasons
To continue and to give back To be strong
for others And myself…
My greatest gifts Are invisible but ever present
so grateful Heaven must be a beautiful place
With you… Be at peace
now mom…
You deserve The best

You will live on in my heart forever…….
Love San 13th August 2023

Mom

Today is Eleven months Since
my world Changed forever...
To love unconditionally Is truly
a gift... You were the epitome
A shining example In caring
In giving with a whole heart...
I miss that mom
Your influence will remain With me
for always
A guiding light That will continue
to glow Helping me To be
the person Who can
represent you... a special honour
Mom... I love you
And
I'm sending you A hug
From me... 13/03/2023

Love San

Mom

Today is one year Since
you left me All of us mom…
And my heart still breaks
Time should be a healer
And maybe it is… But for now
Time is standing still
And I'm missing everything about you….
I will never be the same without you
mom… the pain
Is still there… I know that God is with us And thankful
For
my many blessings… Especially
my Angels
in God's kingdom Working diligently
to keep us safe…
I am grateful knowing You're still present
In your beautiful spirit Lightly tapping

with your heavenly wand to make it better…
I love you mom Knowing that
you're in God's
perfect hands Helps…
Thanks mom For all the special times The smile
on your face The sound of your voice
Will be with me Always….

Love San 13/04/2023

Mom

I miss your hugs
Your smile... Telling me You love me...
That
I can do it... Courageous and brilliant Kind and sweet
You put your trust
And faith In me.... Showered me
With responsibilities And love... Helping me
To stand firm And steady... Preparing me
For something I never wanted
To face... Now I know For sure
Your noble intentions... Sorry mom
But it doesn't Make it easier On my heart...
It is broken In a thousand
Pieces
And I don't know How
To put it

back together Again...
I love you Mom...

San 11/10/2022

Mom

Live free

With a clear conscience And a giving heart

Be unafraid of What lies ahead Because

God is in charge And everything Happens

As it should Sometimes our hearts

Break We wait for

The sun to come Back out...

It's a lonely wait With unimaginable Sadness...

Missing the lights That once shone So brightly...

Now the glow Has dimmed And the clouds

Have set

In the distance... We hope

To see

A ray of light... To illuminate Our paths Once again...

San 25/06/2022

Mom

Thanks For all of Your love And support
All these years... We experienced So
much together... Happiness
To heart ache... Triumphs
And sadness And
so much In between You and I Best friends
Forever
No boundaries Can
Separate Us...
Always A comfort To me
Mom... Being without
you was
Unthinkable... I cannot hug you With
my arms Only in my
Heart And
I am grateful To God

For all His mercies Including
and especially This one...
I love you mom
will always Treasure each
And every day Spent
with you...

Love San
05/01/2024

My sweet mom

My angel in heaven
My source of strength...
I miss your voice your hugs comforting words
sense of purpose mentoring
My safety net... Unseen
But
felt in spirit... I will miss you until the end
Of
my time here on earth... You're still by my side giving me
some consolation... I pray that
you are at infinite peace Now and
someday we will meet Again...

It is now seventeen long months without you...
And I still think about you every single day...

Love always San 13/09/2023

My sweet mom

Another month Has gone
by And I
still miss You so much… My angel
In heaven My best friend
On earth… We were And still are
Inseparable… I love you
Mom For your
Unwavering support… Your caring
Your kindness And your Big heart…
I am insignificant In God's Mighty world
somehow You managed To make me
Feel special… I will
never Forget What you mean
To me… And always Hold you Close
To my heart…

God bless you Mom
In His tender Care…
And save A big hug For me ok…

Love San 13/02/2024

It is now twenty two long months mom…

My sweet sweet mom

You gave me Everything… Your endless
Love Your wise Words… Your gentle
Nudge
In the right Direction… Courage
And confidence To take
The next Step Encouraging me
To conquer My fears When Uncertainty Peers
Through… Making me Stronger With your
unwavering Support
To Believe That I can
Do it You are Amazing And my
Lucky charm Mom…
My blessing From God

I love you So much Mom…

Love San 08/05/2024

Dearest mom

Today is so special Because It is
your day… Earth became More blessed
An Angel Was born… Full of
vitality And love… Caring
And compassion… Showing
That life Is a gift
And possibilities Are endless Once we Believe
That
We can… You mom The perfect Example…
Being positive Was a
Way of life… The
Power of Faith
In the Fulfillment
Of aspirations And dreams Determination
And perseverance Working

In tandem… Most of
All
The love You gave Will never Ever
Be forgotten Mom…
I love you Respect you And thank God For you
Every single Day…
Happy birthday mom And
God Bless you With peace And love Everything you Need
You deserve The best mom My irreplaceable Best Friend
For life…

Love San 06/04/2024

Dad

I never thought I would Be writing this
So soon after Mommy left
But
My best pal Left me Now
I'm all alone No one
to call 'San' to hold
My hand and My heart tight
I love you dad... The place you
Occupy Only reserved
For you... I wish for you
God's endless love And blessings...
And now My two favourite
angels
Are looking over me And I miss you both
So much...

Love always and forever, San
29/05/2022

Dad

My heart aches
When I think Of
your suffering... You had it
Tough... A test of
will And spirit
You soldiered Through it all Physically
It took a toll...
you faced The biggest Challenge of your life
Head on... Like everything
You encountered In this life... never complained
tried To still
make it easier For me
never showing Your pain...
You're something else
Dad... Caring for me
Even when It was difficult
To care
for yourself... I'm realizing
more everyday
Just how special you are... And I love
And respect you even more...
For it....

Love San 31/07/2023

Dad

I don't know How
To start My best pal
For sure... You and I
Riding partners To work
and back... Our short drives...
I miss you so much dad
Your comforting words
Your smile That lights up
your face... Your appreciation
Always... You just being
here With me...
You're irreplaceable Dad...
No one like you
Your room tells your nature...
Intelligence and wisdom Your kindness...
This world Is missing Two of three
Parts That make Me whole...

San 11/10/2022

Dad

Today is another day Without you... To talk to and
to hold your hand... To tell you
How grateful I am
For your dedication... Love and belief in me To sit next
to you... Admiring your strength
And wisdom... To listen
to you Touch another
chord
in my heart I miss you so much dad Time is passing
some things will never change
When it comes
To you... I love you
And thank God for you
Take care Until
we meet again
My sweet Dad...

Love San 29/06/2023

Dad

One year ago I lost my best pal And today
I still miss you so much dad… Not a day
goes by Without
some reminder… Your room This house… Your garden
That you loved so much…
Your favorite brown pants draught board
Your strong hands… Your appreciation
A memory shared between us…
Always being there for me
You made me feel safe… And special
With
your countless Acts
of kindness….
Your presence in my life Will always be sacred…
You now live In
my heart Reminding me of the reason

I'm still here...
I have a purpose
to fulfill A heart to give A dream
to satisfy... An unknown
destiny To reveal...
And although you never asked...
To honor you until
God is ready For me...

I love you And thank God For you dad...

San 29/05/2023

Dad

A treasure Among treasures
Will weather Any storm
For me… will never Forget
dad Everything You did
So grateful… Blessings to last
A Lifetime precious Memories so special
To me… I love respect
And thank God For you
dad
Keep peaceful comfortable
With everything You need Always
Close… God is good taking
Care
Of you now… Thank you
Lord…

Love San 05/01/2024

Dear dad

My protector My mentor My heart...
I miss you So much...
Not a day goes by Without memories Of you dad...
Sad ones And those where
You left footprints Of your wisdom To last
a lifetime... A sense of humor
That lights up a room With laughter...
You're so special To me dad...
Words cannot express God Bless You
In his tender care Now...
I love you dad And thank God for
The precious time We had together
I am truly blessed...

Love San 29/03/2023

Dear dad

You were my sunshine
On a rainy day… My hopes
and dreams… You never faltered
Never wavered… Making me
See myself For what
I can do… You were always There For me….
I miss that dad You are still here
In every room In this house… Your home that
You built with Your own strong hands… Your heart
Will linger here Forever… With me all of us
Who treasure memories That gifted us With
The wisdom Synonymous With you…

What you gave Us
Of yourself No words
To describe… I love you dad
And ever
So grateful… Stay peaceful In God's
Tender care ok…

Love San 29/11/2023
It is now eighteen months And I miss you so much…

Dearest Dad

You would think That after sixteen months My pain of
missing you Will wane... But it hasn't You're
still Ever present In my thoughts
And my heart... Where
I am still keeping You safe...
Your strength
Is what sustained me For my lifetime And I still hang
On ...
If onto only memories Now...
I treasure the times We spent together I respect you
I love you Dad...
And thank God For you Every day...
Rest peacefully And look
Down on me...
Every once in a while ok... Thanks dad
Thanks for everything...

Love San 29/09/2023

Dad

Today is another day Without you... To talk to and
to hold your hand... To tell you
How grateful I am
For your dedication... Love and belief in me To sit next
to you... Admiring your strength
And wisdom... To listen
to you Touch another
chord
in my heart I miss you so much dad Time is passing
some things will never change
When it comes
To you... I love you
And thank God for you
Take care Until
we meet again
My sweet Dad...

Love San 29/06/2023

Dearest dad

I love you miss you respect you And thank God
For you dad… You gave
Of yourself Without
a second Thought… You brought Happiness
and laughter To those fortunate
To know you… You stood strong
And tall With
so much heart… You were my Safety net
You would Catch me if I fall…
You made me See life
As
an opportunity To give…
To be here
In an efficient Way…
To extend myself In an honorable Manner…

Dearest Dad

Today is fifteen months Since you left
And I still feel That you're here…
I see you In my thoughts
And my heart… In your room
In the corridor
In the drawing room In the kitchen Waiting for me
In the workshop In your garden
you loved So much…
Rich with produce You molded With your
Own strong Hands… Exemplifying Your indomitable Spirit…
Wafting through This home This house Forever… Blessing us
Letting us know That perfection Is not
Beyond our reach… Having seen
What perfection Is…

Thanks dad I love you
And miss you

So much…

San 29/08/2023

I still miss you dad

Tomorrow is six months Since
I lost you And not
a day goes by When
I don't think About you… Sadness fills my heart
the tears keep falling… I will never
Get used to this dad…
My prayer for you Is that
You're in a better place Without pain
and discomfort indescribable happiness
goodness
all around you…
In God's tender care… Always
and still looking Down on me from above…
I love you Dad
And I thank God For you…

Love San 28/11/2022

Alzheimer's hurts

Alzheimer's must be one of the most devastating diseases. It takes away your ability to talk eat swallow and builds mucus to a point where breathing is so difficult. Never give up on him because he's still inside this body that doesn't seem to work anymore…He knows that you care and his occasional smile and raised eyebrow is enough to make both of your days. He never stops feeling the love you have for him and the love he has for you…Always let him know that you care in whatever small gesture…a balloon that says happy birthday with meaningful markings… a heartfelt bouquet of flowers from your own lovingly planted garden with a note attached… sitting with him and patiently giving him something to drink no matter how long it takes…gently lifting him to adjust his pillow and tending to his most personal needs with his dignity still intact… tenderly holding his hand…trimming his nails… protecting him from peering eyes and viruses even though it might alienate some…only allowing those who truly care… letting him be the Centre of your world for the time he has left…love him with all of your heart and embrace him with a sense of security knowing that you're near…never far away…

San 21/06/2022

Mom and Dad

My heart Feels
your presence My soul feels your Support
Still...
I know that with you
I am never alone Because God's team Has
grown in strength... You were always
My pillars of hope the forces Behind me
Your encouragement ever present...
I hold on to What
I cannot see But know
Is there... That must be faith

In you And God...
Thanks mom and dad... And thank you God
I am most Blessed.... honored
And privileged
To be your daughter...

Love San 11/05/2023

Mom and Dad

You were my world And now I stand
by myself Though I know
You're still With me in spirit
I miss
Your determination mom
your resilience
dad… Your fearlessness
And
your strength Physical
and mental… I loved that About you…
Happy that you Are
my parents And mentors
In every sense Of the word Reigning supreme Where family
is concerned… exuding
an aura… Encompassing neighbors
Friends and relatives

strangers alike… Where
in this world Exists
such warmth Good nature and goodwill I've yet
to see… Didn't need recognition Just a hug would suffice…
This world Has been truly blessed
with
your presence I am
honored And humbled
To have been Placed in your lifetime You are
My definition of
greatness

Thank you Lord…

Love San 26/05/2023

What we see

On the outside Is most times Not
a true reflection Of what
is inside… Pain is
sometimes hidden From eyes that judge
And observations that hurt… Sometimes
it is better To be seen not heard
To be silent… Be kind
If simply because… Life presents challenges
To everyone No one exempt…
God sees and knows all
He is in charge
of our destiny Not us… We are
His vehicle for
positive change To make this world
better
than we found it To inspire
hope and goodwill In the lives

We are fortunate To touch
in this lifetime He is the only one
who
is perfect
We are the nothings who were
chosen With His mission
of infinite love And
we must always honour this precious responsibility
Just like my two shining
exemplars in humanity
Mommy and daddy... Thank you Lord
I am truly blessed

San 21/03/2023

Nobody sees me...

When
I'm most vulnerable When my tears
fall Silently
on my pillow At night
When my heart is breaking...
When memories flash Before my eyes... And I return to
The saddest days in my life....
The ones that surface every day
Feeling so alone Without you and daddy mom
To console me... To hold me in a hug Like only you can...
To say out loud it's going to be ok... I feel you reaching
out to me
But I cannot touch... To be whole again Is yet to see
There is this fog... I cannot see
Maybe someday... The sun will shine Through...

San 09/02/2023

Thank you Lord

For
my sweet mom Who
I love With all my heart...
Who gave me
More than life...
showed me values Taught me
to care... And
By example Lessons
in humanity... A giving
soul Brightens and perpetuates The flame Of
goodness In others... Resonating
In the Beauty
That surrounds
us... What we don't see
Is sometimes What touches Us
the most... My life is truly blessed

Because you were Here...
God smiled on me
To be your Daughter... Memories Held sacred... Your home
Forever In
my heart...

Love San 13/11/2023

The Lord is my Shepherd

Look forward
with positive thoughts See the future
as a challenge And the present
as a stepping stone Let the flow of life Stimulate new ideas
And create
new opportunities Let us make
an effort to strive With honesty and sincerity
And love For life is short God's will for us
To share and care Give
with a whole heart Put our trust
in Him For
He has
the greatest understanding Of our feelings

Sandra Chatoor 19/08/87

The most beautiful attribute Possessed by anyone
Is their ability
To understand and respect The feelings of others

Peace

A state of mind

A whisper be calm… A gentle Breeze… A divine Guide

To serenity… Floating

On

a cloud Of perfect Silence…

A feathery wisp

From heavenly Angels… To tenderly Land

On solid Ground…

Sandra Chatoor 07/05/2024

Angels

With me Always…
My inspiration To be Good…
To excel In humanity
And Humility… To reveal God given
Gifts Simply…
Purposefully… Leave
A trail
Of kindness
And compassion… To know
I was here Like
My two Angels…
My guides Who
Now reside In heaven…

San 07/05/2024

Being human

Is sharing a meal with a poor and destitute
person…. Is showing others that
Kindness can flourish from within….
Is showing that you care….
Is expressing gratitude….
Is giving a stray pup a bowl of milk….
Is appreciating and being appreciated….
Is being sincere, honest and trustworthy….
Is a pat on the shoulder….
Is a glowing smile….
Is being good-natured….
Is being able to say "I'm sorry"…. Is spreading joy….
Is giving a friendly word of advice…. Is being a friend….
Is complimenting a person for neatness….
Is sending a postcard….
Is sharing a good piece of news….
Is thanking God by being all these things and more!

Sandra Chatoor

God's Gift of Life

Life is lent to us For
a time What
we make of it
Is
up to us squander it…
live it To the fullest… share it
with others… What we do shapes
our destiny… We have
to find our calling pursue it
To
the end… God given talents
To be explored Not discarded
Treasure each second Of
every day make it count For
tomorrow still
but a dream…

15/10/2013 Sandra Chatoor

In the twilight

In the twilight
of each day Just as the sun
is setting... I see
the birds soaring high
in the sky Looking for
a place to rest Their
sleepy heads... They stop
for
a minute On

the trees… quickly flutter their wings daintily dusting
the events Of the day From
their feathers… Surely
A message from God
an example
Of Nature's beauty
And Divinity
surrounding us Just
take a second
to appreciate!

Sandra Chatoor 19/10/2013

Motivation

Should be More than
just obligation... It should be
driven by By heartfelt
caring
And compassion... Risking all
For the ones we love
And those Who need us It should be governed
By the purest of intentions...
Never looking back Moving us
With no regrets... Knowing that we gave our all
No expectations Tapping into hidden strengths
so grateful To discover... It is true that
we give the best Of ourselves When God
is guiding us And our motives
show Who we really are... God Bless

San 20/09/2023

Dedicated to mom and dad I love and respect you
So much….

Parting

Bringing us together
God has indeed been gracious United
In bonds of companionship
loyalty respect
Even the passage of time Doesn't forget.

Unknown to us
Our meeting was planned That's for sure
Never factions or
fragmentations A sense of belonging
We enjoyed life together
peacefully gratefully happily.

But life must go on We must depart

But with pleasant memories Embedded

in our hearts

Never to be

uprooted

Always a comfort.

Our class, each other
Our teachers and Principal,too, We shall remember fondly
With patience and willingness They guided us through.

So, to you,our friends Our advice
Let hard work and compassion Be your goals in life
And success

Not failure Your reward.

Sandra Chatoor

Thoughts to Inspire

Believe in yourself
and anything is possible…

Live with the highest integrity, And your
honesty can never be challenged…

Be humble in your achievements And you will strive better
With the rewards they bring you…

Be compassionate in your dealings And
earn the respect of others…

Speak and act kindly toward strangers
And acquire friends for life…

Be at peace with others, And you will
find peace within yourself.

Sandra Chatoor

Milton Keynes UK
Ingram Content Group UK Ltd.
UKHW042008281024
450365UK00003B/273